# MINUSES:

## all that it takes to avoid calamity?

5 + 5 + 5 + 5

4 + 4 + 4 + 4 + 4

5 - 10 - 15 - 20

20 - 15 - 10 - 5

2 - 4 - 6 - 8 - 10

12 - 14 - 16 - 18 - 20

## GODFREY HOLMES

# © Godfrey Holmes
# January 2021
# ISBN : 978-0-9536016-7-7

*All rights reserved. No part of this publication may be reproduced or transmitted in any form or by any means: electronic or mechanical, including photocopying, recording, or by any information storage and retrieval system- nor may any example be publicly debated word for word – without the prior permission, in writing, from the publisher. A catalogue record of this collection is available from the British Library*

**NETHERMOOR BOOKS**
**"St. Elphin"**
**12 North Promenade**
**Withernsea**
**HU19 2DP**
**Telephone : 01964-615258**

*Contact the Author:*

**godfrey.holmes@btinternet.com**

*The Author - an experienced contributor to Local Radio over many years - welcomes invitations to broadcast at no charge. Apart from Disaster, & Disaster follow-up, Godfrey speaks about Social Work, Truancy, Social Class, Criminology, Road Safety - and Collisions on the Highway.*

*Cover Illustration : © Anna-Maria Dutto*

# TWENTY MINUTES

## Introduction to the Project

---

Years of listening to the News - sometimes obsessively - persuades me that no Government - or Local Government - Inquiry ever ends reassuringly - let alone satisfactorily.

Nearly all these Inquiries speak of evasion, obfuscation & whitewash. Put another way, I cannot trust the Chairperson when he or she appears on the media immediately after an Inquiry's publication saying :

<< *due to a variety of circumstances beyond anybody's control....* >> ... or

<< *we have found serious failings: not attributable to any single officer....*>>... or

<< *in hindsight, the Panel is sure matters would not have unfolded as they did...*>>.... or

<< *undoubtedly this Organization expresses sincere regret - but measures are now in place to avert or avoid or prevent any repeat....*>>

And by the time that same Judge, or whoever, gets round to << Lessons will be learnt," I switch off in frustration, impatience, disgust.

Not infrequently, a *second*, or third, Inquiry has to be held - in view of "new evidence emerging" - & I'm asking why the initial Panel did not unearth these facts or figures?

Public Inquiries are infinitely worse because they take 3, 5, 10, 15, 25 years to report! At a (wasted?) cost to the Taxpayer of millions. Is this a lawyers' bean-feast? Their desired & ultimate Payday? Or are the documents under consideration so plentiful that they fill the cubic capacity of an Olympic Swimming Pool? [ *as really happened when Heathrow Airport wished to expand!* ]

Later I realise - *too late* for the assistance, punishment, or calling to account of incompetent designers, planners or executives lurking at the root of each adverse event, worse each major disaster - those in charge are spared, denied, & are *not seeking*, a few minutes' *forethought*. Time to stand back.

Maybe some despised junior, "troublemaker," back-bench rebel - or whistleblower - *is* prepared to speak out early enough to assure a different outcome - but is not listened to.

Someone has to think outside the box. Beyond the Silo: his or her eyes firmly fixed on their organization's purpose, its reason for existing. Someone should be bothered about impact, side-effects. Somebody needs not to be blinded, distracted, by either expediency or profit.

Now all I have to decide is *how long* that forethought has to be in order to bring about the Holy Grail of "alternative outcome"?

With an unsteady ladder, one minute will be enough. But counteracting, foiling, a complex fraud, forethought might take absorb 3 hours of detailed plan, rôle-allocation & safeguarding.

The truth probably lies somewhere in between. When I first approached the Subject: *ten* minutes  appealed: long enough for efficacy; short enough for a concentration of minds?

Then the number ten lost its glister. Ten minutes could prove irrelevant prior to a chunk of poor decision-making. Ten wouldn't cover the breadth of maladministration I was coming across. So how about *thirty*?

Many shops have a notice in their window: "Back in 30 minutes;" also it's not uncommon to be told by a cobbler or photo-processor: "Pop back in half-an-hour."

Yet, on further reflection, and for my benefit, also every other innocent's benefit, those thirty became too long: unrealistic for the proverbial journeyman embarking on his proverbial journey. Rather too *ponderous* a time-span?

*Twenty*? Yes: Twenty Minutes slips off the tongue. Twenty's a number we often use for baking; for scoring [literally!]; a naughty child's time-out; 5-penny-pieces to the pound; medium-sized orders; & twenty rhymes with "plenty." Not really plenty - but enough, often enough to stand in the way of Calamity: 20 minutes to opt for life instead of death.

***Just 20 Minutes*: the Theme of this Book.**

***TWENTY MINUTES* :**

JUST **20** MINUTES - ***TWENTY*** - while

\*\*\* RECLINING IN A DECK-CHAIR

\*\*\* WAKING UP IN BED

\*\*\* LOUNGING ON THE SOFA

\*\*\* LOOKING ACROSS THE ROAD

\*\*\* PONDERING OVER COFFEE

\*\*\* WAITING AT THE BUS-STOP

\*\*\* ALONE *or* TOGETHER

\*\*\* BEFORE *or* AFTER THAT MEETING

\*\*\* SITTING DOWN for a FAMILY CONFERENCE

\>>> WOULD ACHIEVE THE RIGHT OUTCOME

\>>> WOULD AVOID THE *WRONG* OUTCOME

.......& .... *WOULD AVERT CALAMITY !*

20-20-20-20-20-20-20-20-20-20-20-20-20

# TWENTY MINUTES

## *20 MINUTES*

\*\*\* CONTEMPLATING
\*\*\* SEEKING OUT
\*\*\* SEARCHING
\*\*\* CONSIDERING
\*\*\* JOTTING DOWN
\*\*\* DOODLING
\*\*\* SCRIBBLING
\*\*\* SKETCHING
\*\*\* OUTLINING
\*\*\* MAPPING
\*\*\* THINKING
\*\*\* CHECKING OUT
\*\*\* FEEDING BACK
\*\*\* CONSULTING
\*\*\* MEDITATING
\*\*\* MEDIATING
\*\*\* DECIDING
\*\*\* CALLING
\*\*\* TWEETING
\*\*\* INFLUENCING

# TWENTY MINUTES

### EXAMPLE ONE :

### The DISCHARGE of SICK PATIENTS INTO - or back into - CARE HOMES at the START of CORONA-VIRUS in BRITAIN

*February to June, 2020 -*
at the cost of several thousand excess deaths
[Residents] & countless others [Nursing Staff]

Are we sure every Resident or "Bed-blocker" discharged from Hospital to a Care Home has been thoroughly tested?

Are we sure that, if there's been any outbreak in the Hospital itself, each Patient on the move has been quarantined a fortnight first?

Have we checked that there is no intermediate facility with care brought in: like an empty Hôtel, Army Camp, or post-War Isolation Hospital where our discharged Patients can go for 11 days before entering a Care Home ?

*Just 20 minutes contemplating Outcomes*

# TWENTY MINUTES

## EXAMPLE TWO :

## CONCEIVING A BABY

Imagine the difference : a Baby conceived after 20 minutes - *just twenty* - of that child's future parents talk frankly about their preparedness - or not - to proceed towards Parenthood 1$^{st}$.time, 2$^{nd}$. time - or 3$^{rd}$.

How about the stability of our jobs?
Have we enough Money for another Child in the World - and, tantalizingly:
is the World ready for this addition?
How will our Relationship change?
What about out Hobbies?
Or existing Kinship Ties?
Moreover: have we enough Room in our home [ and our Hearts! ] for a Newborn?

An uncomfortable Conversation -
but never needed more in the midst of - & the wake of - a Pandemic & its ensuing Recession.

*Twenty Minutes of true "Family Planning"*

# TWENTY MINUTES

## EXAMPLE THREE :

## THE ABERFAN DISASTER
## 21$^{st}$. October 1966

*Remembering those 116 people killed:
many of them young School Children:*

Had the National Coal Board spent just 20 minutes studying the huge Coal Tip that was so unstable as to be sliding; or - failing that - if the NCB had spent 20 minutes commissioning another body - other Scientists - to assess possibility of Landslide...*or* had the local County or District Council looked up *the history* of "unforeseen" movements, whether of ice or mud or soot: Aberfan's Disaster of Disasters *might* have been prevented - or if not prevented: halted with time to spare for Mass Evacuation of the Village.

*And Villagers' testimony proves that the Authorities* were *warned... It simply needed 20 extra minutes of LISTENING!*

# TWENTY MINUTES

### EXAMPLE FOUR :

### LIVING TOGETHER ? or LIVING APART ?

This Question was far more abstract before the Corona Virus Epidemic : before hundreds & thousands of would-be Couples were forced to decide whether to become one Household or Two - & for quite a few months....

In pre-Covid days there was a growing trend LTA [ Living Together Apart ] - where some Couples appreciated each other more from the vantage point of two separate addresses.
In turn, this Decision was a by-product of triple phenomena : higher divorce rates; longer Serial Monogamy; plus an unexpected social acceptance of Cohabitation prior to - or instead of - Traditional Marriage.

*Just 20 minutes of earnest Discussion about practicalities - and finance! - similar to a Pre-Nuptial - would iron out very many unpleasant surprises, disputes, wrong turns.*

# TWENTY MINUTES

## EXAMPLE FIVE :

### THE HILLSBOROUGH DISASTER : 12th. April, 1989

So many opportunities were missed to avert one of the worst Football disasters ever, they are almost too numerous to list...
20 minutes would have stopped this F.A. Cup Semi-Final being held at Hillsborough at all. Later, 20 minutes' thought would have furnished Stewards & clear directions.
And 20 minutes' reflection would have halted the erection of high security fences round this - or any other- Pitch. Wicked incarceration.
Pre-Match: 20 minutes would have better prepared the Match Commander for his task.
Finally, far *less than* an extra 20 minutes would have allowed proper Ambulances - & other Paramedics - onto the Pitch.

*[ If only a succession of Home Secretaries had EACH taken 20 minutes more to appoint the right - more diligent & focussed - Judges ? ]*

# TWENTY MINUTES

### EXAMPLE SIX :

### "SMART" MOTORWAYS

Why change Motorways from the way they were first designed over 50 years ago?

What are the *advantages* of dispensing with the Hard Shoulder?
And what are the disadvantages.

And what happens if a vehicle stalls or breaks down in a running lane?
How can other Drivers ever know there's a blockage ahead?

How long is it before motorists receive a message of forward stoppages overhead? Therefore where should the planned rest-bays be positioned? Near enough to other bays?

*Most important, are the* difficulties and dangers *of going "Smart" so overwhelming that it's better to stick with* conventional Motorways? Never is 20 minutes more required.

# TWENTY MINUTES

### EXAMPLE SEVEN:

### MIXED-SEX HOSPITAL WARDS

Regional - or University - Health Boards, also local Hospital Managers, needed only 20 minutes to forestall, then abandon their efforts laying on Mixed-Sex Wards - or those six-, eight-bedded Unisex enclaves Left & Right of Hospital Corridors.

Just 20 minutes of determination would have drawn on Patients' natural reticence to share their Ops, share their pain, share their ablutions, share their toileting, share their gossip, share their medical setbacks - their infections, colostomies, vomiting, screaming - with dressing-gowned Patients of the opposite sex.

So even if the proposition looks right - so sensible! so economic! on paper, *20 minutes make Single-Sex Wards a no-brainer.*

# TWENTY MINUTES

## EXAMPLE EIGHT :

## LOCKING THE COCKPIT DOOR

What are the *advantages* of locking every passenger-aircraft's Cockpit Door?

And who needs to be kept out of the Cockpit at all costs ?

Deciding on "*No Access*" : what type of lock is best : mortice, Yale, or combination?

And what would happen if ever the Cockpit was accidentally or purposefully locked *from the inside*?

Might a simple Code-word or Swipe prove better than physical locking down of the Cockpit?

In all instances: what is the Crew's *or* the Co-Pilot's *override*?

*Saving upward of 150 spree-killings: surely a brilliant use of 20 Minutes!*

# TWENTY MINUTES

## EXAMPLE NINE :

## CRITICIZING A COLLEAGUE'S PERFORMANCE

Were a Line-Manager, Area Manager or Team Leader to stop for just 20 minutes before apprehending or criticizing a Colleague for his or her Performance - or shortcomings - that Boss would quite probably best stay silent; alternatively *reframe* a Colleague's assignment, errand or report as a valuable learning experience. That way: everybody goes home happy & satisfied - *with no loss of face.*

Yet a mere 20 minutes allows a different outcome: some remembrance of who appointed the Colleague *in the first place*; necessary recall of all that Colleague's strengths - as opposed to weaknesses. In turn, those strengths have potential to outweigh, *banish*, a Leader's odd doubts. Line Management is all about filtering out negatives, accentuating positives.

*Twenty Minutes to hold on to a Treasure!*

# TWENTY MINUTES

## EXAMPLE TEN :

## IMAGINING TURNING LEFT ACROSS THE PATH OF A PEDAL-CYCLE

Why are Cyclists *more* at Risk on the road?
What are their comparative chances of
surviving turning Left or Right soon ahead?
How is a *Main* Road different from turning
*out of a Side Road* for the Cyclist ?

When & how is a Cyclist ever *stranded* in the
middle of the road: hemmed in both sides?

Where are likely to be *my* Blind Spots?
Will Pedal-Cyclists be as well protected as me?
And which sudden decisions on my part
will be *most* hazardous for a Pedal-Cyclist ?
And how shall I *communicate* those Decisions?

Lastly. do I have I a good enough Mirror
on my *Nearside*? If so, is it properly adjusted?
How distracted will I be on my commute -
or roundabout journey(s) later to-day?
*Twenty Minutes can save a Cyclist's Life...*

# TWENTY MINUTES

### EXAMPLE ELEVEN :

### BUYING A HOUSE

Is this House in the right place?
And how conveniently is it situated for
the Commute or the School-Run?
Can we walk to local Shops?
What about potentially noisy neighbours?
Think of those high hedges & fierce dogs?

And is the House I'm seeking to buy
meanly or flimsily or carelessly built?
If it's quite an old property: is it draughty :
likely to attract high heating bills.

Of importance: am I being *rushed* into a
speedy purchase decision, maybe off-plan?
Perhaps the asking price is hugely inflated?

Do I *have to* decide before competing
viewings? And what are the chances of selling
this property in years to come?

*Just 20 minutes' more prevarication before the
decade's most important spending decision.*

# TWENTY MINUTES

### EXAMPLE TWELVE :

### SMACKING YOUR CHILD

What has (s)he done wrong?
Does (s)he know that (s)he has sinned?
Has this flare up ever happened before?
Is (s)he simply grizzly, a bit offish, to-day: perhaps getting out of bed on the wrong side?

*Now:* is there any *alternative* to a smack?
How has (s)he responded in the past to threats & actuality?
Could the Naughty Step, or being Grounded - or being set a horrible chore - or having i-phone confiscated - be far more effective?

Finally, shall I be ashamed of resorting to Corporal Punishment? As if it says more about *me* than about my errant child?
Maybe I fear somebody getting to know about it- or telling me it's against the Law?

*At the end of your tether: Twenty Minutes' GAP: so useful!*

# TWENTY MINUTES

### EXAMPLE THIRTEEN :

### ZEEBRUGGE

6$^{Th}$. MARCH, 1987
*The HERALD of FREE ENTERPRISE*
**FERRY OVERTURNS**
**193 PASSENGERS+CREW DEAD**

Is this Roll-On, Roll-Off Ferry completely ready for off?
Has every person & every Vehicle due for boarding actually boarded?

Most important of all: the Bow Door: is it properly shut? And is anyone assigned to *check* that Door is completely closed?

What would happen if we started the Crossing with the ocean flooding the car deck?
Are the waves anything but quiet outside?

Is there any pressure on our sailing To-night because we're behind on timing / loading?

*Just Twenty Minutes delay: to avert Disaster*

# TWENTY MINUTES

### EXAMPLE FOURTEEN :

### BILL-BOARDS ERECTED AT FOOTBALL GROUNDS

Why exactly are we putting up
Advertizing Boards for Football Matches?
What are these Boards meant to sell?
Some Boards Charitable :Virtue Signalling ?
Should not-for-profit Boards be let for less?

What money will Boards bring to the Club?
And - if Boards promote Internet Betting -
what *dis*credit will be heaped on the Club?

Most important of all: will Advertizing Board -
especially electronic & revolving boards -
distract Players & Public alike-
so that fewer folk get a clear view of the Ball?

*Twenty Minutes to stay focussed on our*
*Mission & Reach - with an additional 20*
*needed thinking about our* Shirts?
*What message are* they *sending out?*

# TWENTY MINUTES

## EXAMPLE FIFTEEN :

## DISMANTLING

If I take this Machine or Toy or Appliance
apart, will I be able to re-assemble it?
Has the manufacturer provided a
User's Guide to taking this apart
& putting it back together again?
Am I good at following written instructions?
And have I done anything like this before?

Where will every component-every screw-be
laid? And how good is my labelling / and
numbering? Also, have I got good *eyesight*?

And if the job is going to take "just an hour or
two," is it worth the hassle?
Maybe better to throw the whole compliance
away - and swallow the losses?

*Just 20 minutes might render an
impossibility possible* by another route:
*eg. calling in an expert ?*

# TWENTY MINUTES

### EXAMPLE SIXTEEN:

### CLIMBING THAT MOUNTAIN

How high is this Mountain?
And how *difficult* the Climb ahead?

Who has climbed this Mountain before?
And did they leave any ropes or pegs
or route diagrams behind?

Have I got the skills required for this Climb?
And are these skills usefully supplemented
by a *climbing Companion*?

What will phone reception be up there?
Or any means of alerting base-camp?
In the meantime: what about emergency
provisions or overnight shelter?

Finally, what about the *Descent* if & when
the Ascent has been triumphantly completed?

*20 minutes to look upward - and consider
the still perilous challenge ahead*

# TWENTY MINUTES

### EXAMPLE SEVENTEEN :

### BUNKING OFF SCHOOL

Which Teacher(s) will notice my Absence?
Will a Register be taken: once or thrice?
And will there be any follow-up Telephone
Call home: to check my whereabouts?

Have I ever done anything like this before?
If so what tracks did I have to cover?
And whom did I meet I didn't want to meet?
What *Sickness Letter* did I need to write?
And was there any Punishment or Detention?

Where shall I *go* whilst truanting?
What will I wear if I can dump my Uniform?
And how shall I sink into the background- or
into the crowd without being noticed?

There's certainly comfort in numbers ....
therefore who shall I take with me?

*Maybe I'd be better off arriving in Class
those 20 Minutes late ?*

# TWENTY MINUTES

### EXAMPLE EIGHTEEN :

### GRENFELL TOWER

$14^{th}$. June 2017 :
a conflagration starting with the
malfunction of an electrical appliance
killing 72 trapped Residents :

When was the last Fire Investigation -
& were there any Recommendations to follow?
And when was the last real-life
Fire Evacuation exercise? Day or night?

During Renovation, were all materials used
subjected to sustainability in fierce fire :
with what Testing & what Certificates?

Has the local Fire Brigade got the resources to
attend such a high-rise Building?
With how much water and ladders how high?
In which case, is it worth promoting *Mass
Evacuation*? Far superior to saying: "stay put!"

*20 Minutes to consider* all *eventualities*

# TWENTY MINUTES

## EXAMPLE NINETEEN

## FLOOD PREVENTION

Which Towns & Cities are likely to be flooded after the next heavy rainfall or thunderstorm? Are there any Settlements or Villages situated at *the confluence* of streams or rivers - thus more likely to be completely inundated ?

What would be *the cheapest* way to flood-proof entire Town or Villages? What would be the *most effective* way to flood-proof these Towns, Villages or Shops? Or would Evacuation be the better way? Alternatively: only flood-proof *houses-at-risk* by raising floors - or encasing front doors?

Could widespread provision of flood-barriers adversely affect other settlements further downstream? Or farms & barns on the plain?

*Finally: opportunity to request - demand? - a full cost-benefit analysis.*
*20 minutes balancing risk against return.*

# TWENTY MINUTES

## EXAMPLE TWENTY

## RETIRING FROM WORK

Am I still enjoying my current Employment? Or have I had enough of the job & the bosses?

Am I *hungry* for greater achievements? More challenges? But perhaps this Office or Business cannot not survive without me?

If & when I retired, what would be my monthly income set against my outgoings? Maybe I could live off that money, plus any Redundancy, or Golden Goodbye for many years? Not forgetting my Pension Pot?

Would my *health* improve during early Retirement? Perhaps my Partner & Family would benefit from advancing my Retirement? It could even be my Town or Village would be better served from my extra volunteering?

*Twenty Minutes to get the next 20 Years right!*

# TWENTY MINUTES

## EXAMPLE TWENTY-ONE

### DRIVING IN SNOW

Will the Snow I'll be Driving in be *Falling*
Snow - or Snow compacted on the ground?
Will the Snow ever stop?
Or will it go on & on - and then drift?

Have I had solid experience driving in Snow?
And all the provisions & shovels I'll need?
*First-off*: will I be able to dig the Car out of
my Garage or Drive or away from Roadside?

What are Police & Local Radio Stations saying
about this Snowstorm & the next few hours?

Crucially: how *important* is the Meeting or
Appointment or Gathering I'm heading for?
And will it be cancelled even before I arrive?
Better perhaps to work from home?

*Twenty minutes to avoid the calamity of being*
*stranded, frozen, further delayed - and still*
*lumped with a vehicle to jettison?*

# TWENTY MINUTES

## EXAMPLE TWENTY-TWO :

### GIRLFRIEND SURVIVES HER BOYFRIEND'S SUICIDE

How long have they known each other? And could it be described as a very close & inter-dependent relationship?

Was he a live-in Boyfriend or Stand-Alone? Were his doubts & his worries work-centred or home-centred? *Or inner?*

Now he is dead, will his Girlfriend be embraced by her Parents - his Parents too? - or will her survival, her very existence, be resented by everybody mourning his loss?

What diligent - 24 hour? - supports are now available to this grieving Girlfriend/ Fiancée? And how will her work-place, her friends & her social media links assist her or scare her?

*Twenty Minutes well spent to stop this Girl now take her own Life in sympathy with her dead Lover: a case for discreet Suicide-Watch?*

# TWENTY MINUTES

## EXAMPLE TWENTY-THREE :

### PLANNERS [ Over & Again ] APPROVE ACONCRETE MONSTROSITY FOR HISTORIC YORK

How large will this new Shop or Hôtel or Office Block be? With how many Storeys?

Although a *Concrete* Structure, will it be textured - or clad in wood or brick or stone? How much glass will be used? How reflective? And in what colour?

Will this new building enhance York's ancient Streetscape - or, in some way, *spoil* it? Crucially: can this Building *merge* with all its neighbours - or stick out like a sore thumb?

Most important of all: who will benefit by this edifice being specifically York City Centre? Of such importance as to be in the heart of York rather than put in an anonymous Suburb?

*Twenty Minutes to keep York special...*

# TWENTY MINUTES

### EXAMPLE TWENTY-FOUR :

### WITHDRAWING BENEFITS - or "SANCTIONING" - A YOUNG CLAIMANT NOT IN PAID EMPLOYMENT

How did (s)he get into this position?
When did (s)he last have a job: if applicable?
How and why did (s)he leave / have to leave?

Was (s)he in recent times a NEET ?
( Not in Education, Employment or Training )

Could it be (s)he is sofa-surfing?
Could it be (s)he's being / or had been abused?
Does (s)he have the skills to fill in forms?
And what about the state of Rural Transport?

Most important of all: would denial or deprivation of Benefits leave him or her hungry, destitute or frantic - therefore an *even poorer* candidate for a new opening?

*20 minutes to rescue someone's sanity and insure they do not fall by the wayside*

# TWENTY MINUTES

## EXAMPLE TWENTY-SIX

### ATTENDING AN
### AUCTION OF ANTIQUES

Am I attending as Spectator or as a Buyer?
What is my maximum Budget?
Have I counted Purchase Commission and
transport in my Spending Plan?

What about Preview?
How realistic were items I ticked on Preview?
Is there any chance that what I most desire
is a dud or counterfeit?
Perhaps this item or collection is too small -
*or too big* - for my requirements?

Also, how popular is the Auction I'm up for?
What is its traditional reach?
Does the House specialize in my area of play?

What would I do in the event of a *Bidding War*: one hastened by Guide Price(s)?

*Twenty Minutes to disentangle myself*

# TWENTY MINUTES

### EXAMPLE TWENTY-SEVEN

### AVERTING THE WINDRUSH SCANDAL
### 2010 to 2020

What years were the peak for West Indian - & Afro-Caribbean immigration into Britain?

What promises - or assurances - were made by the then Government to the then newcomers?

Also what gaps in this country's Labour Market was it intended incoming breadwinners should fill - if at all practical ?

How well did these new populations integrate in *established* Towns, Cities & Communities?

Of great importance: will every single "Immigrant" or, nowadays, "2$^{nd}$. Generation Immigrant" have enough Paperwork to *prove* they were aboard the *Windrush*? In which case, could *partial* evidence plus interview suffice to prove eligibility to stay?

*Just Twenty Minutes to prevent Re-patriation*

# TWENTY MINUTES

## EXAMPLE TWENTY-EIGHT

### PREPARING FOR A FUTURE PANDEMIC

When was the last Pandemic - and did it prove as lethal & terrible as predicted?

What class was the last Pandemic: Scourge, Food Poisoning, Virus, Infection, VD?

What products should we *stockpile* for the next Pandemic - whenever & wherever it is: Gloves, Masks, Gowns, Towels, Sheets?

Would it be wise to take a punt and train several thousand more Nurses than we require just now? Also 100s of Care Workers?

How frequently should we convene our Pandemic Task Force(s) - and what arrangements are in place to keep these Teams on high alert? Also updated?

*Twenty Minutes to think the unthinkable; Twenty Minutes to store up a Treasure Chest*

# TWENTY MINUTES

## EXAMPLE TWENTY-NINE

### PAINTING THE OUTSIDE OF MY HOUSE IN BOLD & DISTINCTIVE COLOUR

*Key Consideration*: is my house or property in a Conservation Area or within boundaries where the Local Authority is likely to be choosy as to Colour?

Will I need Planning Permission?

If it is left to *me* what colour to choose: will that colour blend with other cottages or larger houses nearby that have been rendered?

Could my Property soon appear a flaking eyesore? Sticking out like a sore thumb?

Maybe it is worth asking my Neighbours for their opinions?

Finally, I could commission an artist's impression, indicating invisible blend?

*Twenty Minutes to save a lot of time & trouble*

# TWENTY MINUTES

## EXAMPLE THIRTY

### JOINING A LATE- EVENING BINGE - or DRINKING PARTY

How much Alcohol have I already consumed this evening or to-day?

Do I keep a Drinks' Diary? And do I fill it in with honesty? What about Alcohol-free?

Am I going out for eating, drinking, eating *and* drinking - or for socializing?
And, if socializing: are these really folk I am pining to meet - so will benefit from meeting?

If there is a Round, who will pay for that Round - & in what order? Perhaps I & a few others end up with the larger/ or largest bill?

Finally, how do I think I'll feel *at the end* of to-night? Perhaps full of regrets: languid, hazy, uncomfortable, sick & nauseous?

*Twenty Minutes to emerge with dignity*

# TWENTY MINUTES

## EXAMPLE THIRTY-ONE:

## RESIGNING VOLUNTARILY

What's driven me - or forced me - to the juncture I have to ask that question?

When was the last time I felt really satisfied at work: sure my contribution is valued?

Could the company or firm or organization I'm already part of continue without me?

Are there any particular friendships / relationships I have been privileged to form in my employment that would be lost through resignation? And can these be replicated - even perpetuated - upon my moving on?

Most important: are my skills attractive, marketable & transferable enough to obtain as good a position & income in another setting?

*Twenty Minutes not to be stuck in the middle of life's stream without a paddle*

# TWENTY MINUTES

### EXAMPLE THIRTY-TWO:

### DECIDING NOT TO HOLD A SNAP GENERAL ELECTION IN THE AUTUMN OF 2007

Is less than half-a-year long enough for me and my Government to illustrate we're all doing a splendid job?

What have been the Policy & *Outcome* triumphs of both my Administration - & that voted into office at the 2005 General Election?

Does it matter if the wider Electorate never actually voted for *me* as their Prime Minister? Indeed, can the general public ever vote for their Premier - or only for their local M.P.?

If we go the Country well before Christmas: have we an attractive enough package to present to the Electorate?

Finally, are there any *downsides* to holding back from seeking a new Mandate?

*Twenty Minutes to act decisively*

# TWENTY MINUTES

## EXAMPLE THIRTY-TWO

### SENDING A LETTER
### TO MY LOCAL NEWSPAPER

How involved, how frustrated, how angry indeed, am I about the issue I want airing?

Have I already exhausted all the channels available to me: short of presenting these matters to a much wider Audience?

Or if my Letter to the Editor is one of *thanks*, is that thanks deserved? Alternatively, could fulsome thanks make me look fawning?

Going back to criticism: have I thoroughly checked all my facts & figures, exhaustively enough to be able to stand by my calculations if challenged?

Most important: should I send this Letter in anonymously *or credited*? And *if* I'm readily traceable: will there be a brick through the window - lots of simmering resentment ?

*Twenty Minutes debating "all publicity good"*

# TWENTY MINUTES

## EXAMPLE THIRTY-FOUR

### GOING OFF TO UNIVERSITY FAR AWAY FROM MY HOME TOWN

What has my Family - or adopted Family - done for me these past 17 years or so?

What has this Town or City done for me and my class these past 17 years or so? Perhaps my Town needs Presentees for *it* to survive?

Do I belong to any Church or Mosque or Choir or Sports' Club - or Movement - solely based here, which I would miss if I went away?

Which close friends / friendship groups would I have to desert or lose touch with?

And *if* I go far away, how often am I likely to be travelling back home?
Or perhaps I'll start a brand new life far away?

*Last of all: is it economically preferable for me to go to a distant University right now?*

# TWENTY MINUTES

## EXAMPLE THIRTY-FIVE

### INCLUDING A DAMNING FACT or ADMISSION or MISDEED or OMISSION in a BIOGRAPHY READY TO PUBLISH

Am I the Author, the joint Author, Collaborator or lead Contributor for this Biography / or ghosted Autobiography?

How did I come across, or trace, or unearth, or recall this particular incident or event?

Is it a fact or episode the person(s) being written about had striven earnestly to hide or conceal from the outside world?

Would my writing about this sting, these feet of clay, make me feel less good about myself or my Collaborators? Could I sleep at night?

*Most important of all*: would publication cause commotion, challenges, recriminations, bitterness, so diminishing me & my Subject?

*Twenty Minutes to set the record straight?*

# TWENTY MINUTES

## EXAMPLE THIRTY-SIX

## OUTING a TRADER or RETAILER

What exactly has this Business done that is illegal, immoral or illegitimate?

On a Scale of 1 to 10, how wrong or harmful or dishonest was this deed/ misdeed?

Did the Owner/ Manager give me chance to discuss this issue *privily*: with an understanding that repair or reform - even dismissals - might follow in due course?
In which case, do I believe this person, or the Board & their reassurance(s) ?

Would my reporting and outing of this Trader put him or her out of business forever?
In which case: is my act of outing fair?

During the act of outing or pursuit or whistle-blowing, is there part of me that wants reward, gratitude, recognition, compensation?

*Twenty Minutes to fine-tune the fire-power*

# TWENTY MINUTES

## EXAMPLE THIRTY-SEVEN

## DESTROYING a WEDDING PHOTO or a WEDDING ALBUM

What is my motivation for throwing this particular photograph or album into the waste-bin or the fire?

Could I wake up tomorrow or in a few days or weeks' time & regret this act of destruction?

Could it be another Couple, Friend or Neighbour is included in the periphery of one of the Group Photos: so destruction would destroy memories of them, their relations too?

Could it be I store this Photo or Album somewhere dry, safe & secure so that, if ever in the future I needed or wanted it, it would still be in existence? Ready for the "new me."

*Most important: is destruction really the re-awakening of my Anger/ or Resentment better dealt with perhaps in another way?*

# TWENTY MINUTES

## EXAMPLE THIRTY-EIGHT

### DONATING a MEMORIAL BENCH to the LOCAL COUNCIL / or TRUST

Who is meant to be memorialized: my Loved One... *or me*?

When did I last pass along the pathway I have selected for this Memorial Bench? ... and crucially, what state were *existing* Benches in when last I passed that way?

Further, was that series or cluster of Benches adorned with photos, toys, cards, flower-vases, ribbons, shirts or other funerary memorabilia? And how did that make *me* respond, especially when I sat down on one of these Benches?

What wording shall I choose for the Plaque - & will that be the start *or end* of years or decades of my tending to that Bench ?

*Twenty Minutes seated to await future seating......*

# TWENTY MINUTES

## EXAMPLE THIRTY-NINE

### INTENTION to DEMOLISH A CHURCH - or NONCONFORMIST CHAPEL?

When exactly was this Place of Worship built? And why erected in *this particular* Village or Town or City Suburb? & is it *still* central?

If built by a land-owner or major donor, *who was* he or she? With any living descendents?

Do any Registers or Records exist numbering this Church's Congregation on Easter Sunday? Feast Days? or Sunday School Anniversaries?

When did this Church or Chapel close for Public Worship - or dwindle away? and *Why*?

If permitted: could this structure ever be profitably converted into apartments, office space, a Bar, a Museum - or a single dwelling?

Perhaps save remarkable façade by itself?

*Twenty Minutes to pray for a solution*

# TWENTY MINUTES

## EXAMPLE FORTY

### THE BRADFORD CITY STADIUM FIRE
### May 11$^{Th}$., 1985

How many fans are expected this afternoon?
How many home fans? How many "away"?

When - if ever? - was a full evacuation of this
Stadium practised? And was this a *staged*
experiment - or in real Match-day conditions?

Are all the Exits clearly marked & escape-
routes to reach them? Do doors open *inwards*?

Will any smoking or vaping or Fireworks be
allowed this afternoon? Or hooliganism?

*Crucially*: when was all that accumulated
rubbish last swept-up & taken to the Tip?

*Twenty minutes to save 56 people killed - with
another 265 injured, scorched, scarred -
& traumatized for Life. Looking back 35 years:
still twenty of the most unused minutes ever...*

# TWENTY MINUTES

## EXAMPLE FORTY-ONE

### ATTENDING A PUBLIC DEMONSTRATION

What am I planning to protest about?

Is this a *March*: where Banners, Slogans & Keynote Speeches will be the best way of Protest? Who is the Organizer?

Will any Government or Governance ever listen to me or to 100s of other Protesters?

What happened to me - & those around me - the last time I attended a Public Rally?

What food, drink, toileting, sleep do I need - or must acquire? And which musical instrument?

Key consideration: is there realistic prospect of opponents, disrupters, stirrers, infiltrators & plain-clothes' Policemen joining our Protest so that it's comprehensively trashed? Emasculated

*20 minutes on the sidelines or in the fray*

# TWENTY MINUTES

## EXAMPLE FORTY-TWO

### STAYING UP ALL NIGHT TO COMPLETE A DIFFICULT JIGSAW

Just how much of a Challenge has this Jigsaw proven to be already? *Is it do-able?*

Will another 5 or 6 hours actually solve those areas I am finding impossible?

Does it *matter* if this Jigsaw is not completed to-night or this week? Or ever?

Have I any place or means to store the part(s) or the canvas I have completed so far?

Moreover, were I to get through towards completion through the night hours, might my Concentration lapse : worse the Endeavour ruin my driving, my functioning, the quality of my relationships and output on the morrow?

*Twenty Minutes to downsize - & put to bed! - an Obsession*

# TWENTY MINUTES

## EXAMPLE FORTY-THREE

## DELIVERING A DAMNING FAREWELL SPEECH AT THE LEAVING-DO

How important is the Person - or myself - who is leaving this body or organization?

How fundamental is it that I grasp *this* occasion to tell the full Story? Clear the decks?

Who knows the Story *already* - so that the majority of people do not need its repetition?

Could all the points I wish to make be better made - perhaps more influentially? - at a private Supper, in the Pub later, or by Letter?

Whose day, or evening, or memory or stability- whose employ? - will I impact upon, *or ruin*, by going ahead to deliver this Speech?

*And key to my eventual Decision,* well worth 20 minutes: *is this the sort of Body or Firm or School or Office which will change its ways or its policies* after *my Contribution?*

# TWENTY MINUTES

## EXAMPLE FORTY-FOUR

### JOINING A PONZI SCHEME

How much money have I got to spare - or *not* got to spare - to lead me to be tempted?

How much Interest are these Savings making already - & with what room for withdrawal?

Is my fascination with Ponzi born of a Cold Call - or follow-up to a dodgy Cold Call?

Which named - & *traceable* - person or body is behind this "Fine Investment?"

Is there any foreign acquisition or shell ownership of this asset: be it fine wine, an ostrich-farm, storage-container, Hôtel, stamp-collection or sundry investment vehicle?

What laws or financial protections surround this type of Investment or location?
And if I'm among *the first*, richest, Investors, what will befall later, less-shielded, punters?

*Twenty Minutes to choose caution above profit*

# TWENTY MINUTES

## EXAMPLE FORTY-FIVE

### GOING ROUND TO SOMEBODY'S HOME IN ORDER TO RESOLVE A DISPUTE

How well do I know the Parents, or Friends of a Friend, that I'm going round to tackle?

What is so urgent / so upsetting about what has gone wrong / likely to go wrong?

Does this Dispute involve Children - in which case they'll defend any Child vigorously?

Will this Family be eating, watching a Soap, sleeping - or about to retire - when I arrive?

What about Home Advantage?
Would it have been better to invite them *here*?

Is there any Script I could employ or read out to make this Confrontation less contentious?

How about ringing, writing a Letter - or simply burying the matter altogether?

*Twenty Minutes to circumvent a skirmish*

# TWENTY MINUTES

## EXAMPLE FORTY-SIX

## TURNING DOWN AN HONOUR

How have I merited promise of an Honour?
And should it honour *me* - or be an Honour for
the Organization / Society I represent?

Is this a pukka Honour: one really worth
acquiring - or a mere trinket?

Is it the sort of Honour I'd put on my headed
notepaper &incorporate in my domain?

If I accept this Honour, will it be an ego-trip:
*glory to me, glory to me*?

Turning this Honour down: would that gesture,
that Sacrifice, *also* be Self-Enhancing?
*When* turned down, is it the sort of Honour that
could come round *again* in the fullness of
time? Or does my snub stick? Always recited?

*Twenty Minutes to consider how this Honour
will look in a year or two's time:
stepping-stone to further aggrandisement?*

# TWENTY MINUTES

### EXAMPLE FORTY-SEVEN

### DECIDING WHETHER TO JOIN A COMMUNITY CHOIR

Do I love singing enough to sing in quite a big Choir?
And am I *patient* enough to know that I might be singing next to untrained voices?

Have I got the time for all the Rehearsals, then the Performances,
then our visits to Elderly Persons' Homes?

Am I likely to enjoy the Repertoire: which might be filled with "lightweight" music: Songs from the Shows, American Smug, Love Songs.... or Gilbert & Sullivan?

Conversely, will I be *sure enough* of my faith to sing Carols, Hymns, Canticles & Masses?

If I want to leave almost as soon as I've joined: is that fair? Will I *hate* the gossip & intrigue?

*Twenty Minutes to strike the right note*

## EXAMPLE FORTY-EIGHT

## RELEASING A MOTHER WHO HAS KILLED HER CHILDREN

Why would *any* Mother kill her own children?
Does it take a particular set of pressures or
debts - psychosis - to kill your birth children?

Are there any extenuating circumstances for
*this* Mother: abuse? duress? mental instability?
carbon monoxide? inadvertent neglect?

Did this mother have a bad, deprived or cruel
childhood herself? And her later attachments?
Who is her *co-accused* - if he exists?

Will there be revenge - reprisals - in her home
town once this woman is released?

So will she need a new identity?
And what will happen if she has more children
[replacement children ]?

*Twenty minutes is never long enough to cram*
*in all the pluses and minuses of taking all*
*those risks, releasing someone so damaged*

# TWENTY MINUTES

### EXAMPLE FORTY-NINE

### THE OPPORTUNITY TO WATCH REALLY EXTREME HARDCORE PORN

Is this material I would be proud for my spouse or child or brother or sister or employer or close friend to be happy knowing I view?

Will this material "educate" me on a Subject I do not fully understand? Conversely: could it debase me & feeding me images I cannot rid?

Is it actually *criminal* to access this material? Alternatively, did criminals put it together?

Once on my Computer or Computer Memory will my accessing it ever be erased?

Which women or children or animals had to be compromised for this material to be on tap?

*Twenty Minutes is probably too long to reach a decision not to touch this with a barge-pole: so great the chance of corruption...*

# TWENTY MINUTES

## EXAMPLE FIFTY

## POLICE DECIDING TO STOP-&-SEARCH

What exactly has this person or vehicle done wrong: wrong enough to be stopped?

Is the misdeed, miscalculation, mistake or mis-speak one that would *normally* warrant a more detailed enquiry? Is this why I joined up?

Has there been a recent outbreak of violence, drug-dealing or anti-social behaviour?

Is the person I'm about to search black? In which case, was the last person I stopped also black? What is my Force's policy on stopping black suspects? And are local communities alienated: enough to *provoke* conflict?

When I *last* stopped a BEM suspect/ or driver, did either (s)he or I gather this was racist? Maybe I've simply suppressed my prejudice?

*Twenty Minutes' time out to let this opportunity pass - even if it's the wrong call?*

# TWENTY MINUTES

### EXAMPLE FIFTY-ONE

### NOT BOARDING AN UNSAFE PLANE

Is my fear, this time, a fear of an unsafe aeroplane - or fear of flying: any flying?

When was this make of aeroplane last on fire, unable to take off - or crash-landing?

How many people were killed or injured? And were the regulatory authorities the least bit attentive, thorough - *or independent*?

Is my fear partly fear of my intended *Airport/* or Airstrip? Surrounded by high mountains? Chaotic? Subject to lax local controls?

What *other* things have gone wrong apart from failed engines? Hatches? Inexperienced crews?

And is there any other method, perhaps overland, getting to my chosen destination?

*No to this plane, in particular, lessening the prospect of personal Disaster immeasurably*

# TWENTY MINUTES

## EXAMPLE FIFTY-TWO

### WHETHER TO DELIVER A FUNERAL ORATION

Am I the best person / relative / or friend to deliver this Oration / Appreciation?

Will *other* relations or friends feel excluded if I deliver the Oration - instead of they?

Has the Funeral Director / Officiator left enough *time* for a proper Appreciation?
If not, might that Appreciation be better incorporated into a Memorial Pamphlet?

Am I entirely sure I can get through the whole Service / or Ceremony without tears?
Will tearfulness affect my delivery?
In which case, could I write the full text & leave it to somebody else to do the talking?

*Most apposite: is this Oration or Appreciation what the deceased person would have wanted, including faults & downsides in the mix?*

# TWENTY MINUTES

## EXAMPLE FIFTY-THREE

## TAKING a PROBABLY - or POTENTIALLY - FATAL OVERDOSE

By my even stopping for a few minutes before doing it: does that indicate I'm still unsure?

Is my intention to take these tablets a gesture about Life, not Death? In other words, am I trying to send a Message - a strong Message - to a *living* person or family or employer?

When - if ever - did I last make an attempt on my life? And what were the consequences?

Is there anybody - anybody at all? - like a neighbour a sister - or the Samaritans - that I could possibly talk to before this Overdose? Is there, as alternative: a walk, or day-trip, even a Seaside Holiday, I could enjoy before doing what I intend to do? Totally *different* stimuli?

*Twenty minutes: amazingly sufficient, in the order of things, to halt a headlong - headstrong? - rush towards hospital or death.*

# TWENTY MINUTES

## EXAMPLE FIFTY-FOUR

### GOVERNMENT ASSISTANCE for a FLOODED TOWN or VILLAGE

Is this Calamity - this Inundation - so grave, so widespread that the Local Authority cannot tackle it without national Government?

Is this Calamitous Inundation beyond a competent Fire & Rescue Service's response?

How much extra money is needed for blankets, tents, caravans, day centres, Church Halls, grocery deliveries - also garbage retrieval? And will this extra money be needed over some months *after* this week's Emergency? And *if* the Government steps into one Town or Village's plight: will that set an unrealistic expectation the State will be there next time?

*When, so often, Government hesitates or falters intervening: where is primary responsibility: making this Apocalyptic Flood so demanding of action? 20 minutes' head above water...*

# TWENTY MINUTES

## EXAMPLE FIFTY-FIVE

### TELLING an ABUSIVE BOYFRIEND TO LEAVE - or *YOU* WILL BE THE ONE GOING

Is my decision to change this Co-habitation based on weeks, months &years of cruelty & tyranny - or one day, one dreadful event?
In the latter case, was that one day / one event grave enough to still warrant quitting?

If I tell my Boyfriend to get the Hell out: is he likely to go willingly? And does he need to take simple things like a bed, or pay-off, or white-van, in order to leave this house / or flat?

Is my Boyfriend unstable, quarrelsome & violent enough to assault - *& probably kill* - me immediately I break the bad news to him?
In which case, might I be better - *& safer* - not to say *anything* at all till I'm gone?

*20 minutes before I leave my primary residence & all my possessions, my rights, my security - inviolability - never to have them back again?*

# TWENTY MINUTES

## EXAMPLE FIFTY-SIX

### PLANNING TO BUILD A BLOCK OF HOUSING ABOVE TEN STOREYS HIGH

If I plan this Block - or offer backing to a builder-client - does it have to be quite this height upon occupation?
Is this the best use of the land we've earmarked- & is this plot anywhere near *other* high-rise blocks or developments?

Above ten-storeys, how will the Lifts work? Which Lift is *least* likely to fail? Should I perhaps put in for two, three, separate Lifts?

In case of fire - or my block being hit by storm or aeroplane: would calm, sensible evacuation be ever possible - or remotely realistic?

*And what quality of life am I offering for individuals or families living & working; looking after children or amusing those children; caring for elderly or infirm relatives above that crucial threshhold of ten storeys?*

# TWENTY MINUTES

## EXAMPLE FIFTY-SEVEN

### TO DRESS DOWN FOR AN INTERVIEW

What manner & fashion of dress makes me most comfortable for this Interview/ Meeting?

What manner & fashion of dress makes *other people* at my Interview or Meeting more at ease - as far as I can tell at this juncture?

Do I want to make a statement by dressing as I will: a statement, perhaps, about (in)formality?

Could I *lose* a future job, contract or agreement - or lose credibility - by calling it my way? Could, or should, I ask for some guidance: even ringing up the Venue to check?

In the mirror, do I look *consistently* good: good enough for me to shine whilst those looking me up-&-down go straight onto the next formality without being held back by my dress choice?

*When compared with going out for a Date or a Dance: twenty minutes is inconsequential*

# TWENTY MINUTES

## EXAMPLE FIFTY-EIGHT

### OFFERING TO BE a WITNESS
### to a CAR or CYCLE COLLISION

Were there other people or vehicles there to give just as good a Testimony as mine - or better? In which case: can I give a Witness Statement from a slightly different angle?

Have I *time* & recall enough to make a Witness Statement to-day: depending on nearness to a Police Station with a counter?
And if I *do* possess that time & that recall: will I be welcomed making a Statement?
And could that voluntary gesture / or obligation be followed up with a lengthy Trial?

Chasing a hare: what might be the outcome if *nobody* gets to speak to Police; if *nobody* stops at the Scene? And how does those omissions leave an injured *or innocent* victim? R.T.A.?

*Just twenty minutes' determination on my part might be the missing piece of a jigsaw...*

# TWENTY MINUTES

## EXAMPLE FIFTY-NINE

### SELLING ON A DUD MOTOR CAR

What sort of problems - big or small - have *I* had with this motor since purchased new?

Have any of those faults, failures or problems been small enough *not* to declare to a future purchaser? Perhaps jeopardizing their safety?

Were I to sell it "*as seen*" to a Second-Hand Car Dealer, would *that* release me from any obligation to recite a full history of problems?

And if I sold it by small Newspaper ad: would I be far happier informing him / or her - maybe a teenager, a first-time buyer - the majority of this, discounted, car's defects? Or could I - *should I?* - consider an Auction?

*So* in *my allocated twenty minutes' thought, I must consider not only how much money I can make* - or avoid spending - *but also due diligence; & that dreaded knock on the door when my purchaser discovers the truth....*

# TWENTY MINUTES

## EXAMPLE SIXTY

## RESISTING TEMPTATION

What exactly am I being tempted to do, or hear, or say, or *not do* - when I ought to do it?

What was the last time I was similarly tempted? And how did I respond?

Looking back from this vantage-point: did I sense it to be, or did that emerge as, the best & proper response?

What might be the consequence(s) now, or later, of *surrendering* to Temptation? And do any of these outcomes hurt or betray others?

Maybe there is a *halfway* house: yielding to this Temptation via a very different route: more positively? more creatively? - so finding satisfaction / & peace of mind another way?

*Reacquainting myself with those 20 magic Minutes - just 20! - to turn my back on whichever gremlin or devil is tormenting me*

## EPILOGUE - or AFTERNOTE

My whole thesis - my whole proposition in this book - centres on my - your ? - our ? - complete dependence on Twenty Minutes: 20 minutes' suspense; 20 minutes' gap; 20 minutes to consider - or re-consider - both an existing state of affairs, then future outlook.

Happily, back-story *and* prospectus will be entirely positive. But in real life, there are shortfalls, omissions, mistakes, false leads: either side of stock-take.

If- & *it is a big if* - my theory of 20 minutes works, it succeeds or fails with absence or presence of a *Guiding Mind.*

The notion of Guiding Mind is not yet incorporated in legislation or rules of governance, or departmental procedures. In fact 100s of Charities, Businesses, Suppliers, Retailers, even Small-&-Medium sized Enterprises are glad, relieved indeed, there is *no* Guiding Mind. In which case, nobody, *nobody at all*, can get the cop or the chop....

The best Guiding Mind is *Self*. So it follows most of my 60 examples are very personal. Self can do one thing. Self can do the other. Self can weigh up hazard. Or Self can *ignore* hazard

Only a minority of my 60 examples deal with the macro rather than the micro. That's because no Guiding Mind will willingly - *or ever* - come forward, even if suspected, vainly taken to Court or Tribunal. Then *inevitably* acquitted.

So, here, my argument for 20 minutes has to rely on an *outsider* : an inspector, ombudsman, adjudicator, newspaper reporter, former employee, referee - *or passer-by* - identifying himself or herself *in place of* Guiding Mind.

Here the law *does* help. The law either awards this outsider the right to intervene, maybe suggest or encourage, improvement - even garner full review of practices & procedures. Leading to a commotion, a hubbub: internally, externally, with the promise of *change*.

Alternatively, and in the absence of strictly formal assessment, the law provides for: " the man on the top of a Clapham Omnibus": another name for the preacher's "man in the street." This mythical character is the *yardstick* against which all reasonable and sensible decision-making should be judged.

No Clapham Omnibus: no plumb-line. Nor any proof of guilt - innocence? - *"beyond the balance of probability."*

So, in Conclusion, I ask *everyone* picking up this book to be that 20-minuter. Constantly to be on your guard & on your alert. *Never fearing to speak truth to power.*

Because you have been born - positioned - in one time & one place: to be a Messenger; to be the little boy who perceives the Emperor is without his clothes.

*Just Twenty Minutes.*

20-20-20-20-20-20-20-20-20
20-20-20-20-20-20-20-20-20-20-20

**OTHER RECENT BOOKS BY GODFREY HOLMES :**

**THE LINE- STORY**
*The Nation's Newest Pastime*
978-0-9536016-2-2

**YOUR CONVERSATION - OR MINE ?**
*200 Tactics When Talking*
978-0-9536016-0-9

**A DICTIONARY OF OPPRESSION IN THE WORKPLACE**
978-0-9536016-5-3

**A DICTIONARY OF TRUANCY**
978-0-9536016-6-0

**SANDCASTLES DO NOT FALL**
*New Holderness Verse*
978-0-9536016-4-6

**VEHICLE IN COLLISION**
What did you see?
978-0-9536016-9-1

**WITHERNSEA: A SENSE OF PLACE, A PLACE OF SENSE**
Limericks for the Lighthouse
978-09934644-4-7

**TANGLED WRECKAGE:**
*An Encyclopaedia of Collision on the Public Highway*
978-09934644-1-6

*All available from*
*Nethermoor Books, telephone : 01964-615258,*
*or at your Local Bookshop -*
*or from Waterstones Online - or via Amazon*

**ENTER HERE *YOUR* PERSONAL LIST
of EVENTS or OCCASIONS
WHERE *YOU* THINK 20 MINUTES
COULD HAVE MADE
ALL THE DIFFERENCE:**